LIFE ADVICE FROM A

Snarky Scorpio

FIONA JEFFERIES

Copyright © 2020 by Fiona Jefferies.

All rights reserved. No part of this publication may be reproduced, distributed or transmitted in any form or by any means, including photocopying, recording, or other electronic or mechanical methods, without the prior written permission of the publisher, except in the case of brief quotations embodied in critical reviews and certain other noncommercial uses permitted by copyright law. For permission requests, write to the publisher, addressed "Attention: Permissions Coordinator," at the address below.

Fiona Jeffferies

PO Box 602

Lane Cove 1595 NSW Australia

Ordering Information:

Quantity sales. Special discounts are available on quantity purchases by corporations, associations, and others. For details, contact the "Special Sales Department" at the address above.

Life Advice from a Snarky Scorpio/ Fiona Jefferies —1st ed.

Author Photo ©Sol+Co

ISBN 978-0-646-83090-2

Dedicated to all the people who aren't Scorpios. I'm sorry for your loss.

Also dedicated to G who got to hear this advice live and in person. How unbelievably lucky you are.

INTRODUCTION

It's typical for an author—especially in the realm of advice—to provide bona fides to prove the self to the reader that they are indeed qualified to offer advice.

All you need to know about me can be summed up in two points.

1. I am and have been a Scorpio Sun for 49 years with the meter still running. For an added kick, that Scorpio Sun in is my 12th House and I also have Scorpio Rising. For anyone not au fait with astrology, that means I'm a lovely person, and I look stunning in a tweed skirt and pearls.

2. At five years of age, two major life events occurred that set me up for the light-hearted life of a Scorpio. Firstly, I won 2nd place in the "Cuddliest Soft Toy" category at my school fete for my Holly Hobbie doll my Aunty Christine made for me by her hand. That second-place taught me it's desirable to be underestimated in life, even in the realm of soft, cuddly toys. Bitches won't see you coming.

2a. The other life-altering event occurred when I was

having my tonsils and adenoids out in a hospital. I was clad in a paper hospital gown, waiting on a trolley with a thin mattress with Holly Hobbie beside me.

Pleasant lady nurse comes to me, ready to push the trolley to the operating theatre and says that I need to remove my underpants from under my paper gown. What? No way, I think. I have my very best knickers on with the sweet floral embroidery across the top elastic edge. If I take them off, who's to say if I'll see them again. But also, and more importantly...why do the knickers come off when even I, as a 5-year-old, know my tonsils and adenoids aren't even in the adjoining neighbourhood of my knicker area?

So, I proceed to reign hell down on pleasant lady nurse in that packed ward, as only a 5-year-old with her very best knickers on, can. And, dear reader—those knickers stayed ON!

The takeaway from this is that I learned from a young age to question stupid things people say or ask. I also learned to practise discernment when it comes to removing one's knickers. Just because you're asked, doesn't mean you have to yield to that shit.

So, with the bona fides in place...let's roll bitches!

DO the fucking thing you keep putting off. Because:

   A. You'll feel that sweet feeling of relief.

   B. You'll feel like a smug bitch because you got shit done.

   C. It's taking up significant bandwidth finding things to do so that you avoid the thing you need to do.

SAY it. Say it even though it will break someone's heart. Say it even if it will disappoint someone. Say it even though you don't know how the other person will respond. Say it even though your voice trembles and you feel like emptying the contents of your stomach onto your most excellent heels. Say it even though the repercussions are known. Say it because—sweet cakes—all we have in the end is the truth.

THEY don't love you. Love does not carry the banners of meanness, disrespect, coldness, wavering attention and violence before it. If it's causing you pain in your heart, sleeplessness, your words to stay stuck in your throat or you recoil at their touch, your body knows what you're unwilling to acknowledge. It ain't love, and you'd be best extracting yourself from whatever situation that makes you feel this way.

TORCH everything behind you. When a relationship is over, it's done. Revel in its finality. Do not seek to resurrect the abandoned corpse of a relationship, no matter how good the sex/food/conversation/view from the shared condo was. It's over. You have new seas to set sail on.

NOSTALGIA is a form of inertia. The most tedious people on the planet are those who pine for a time that never existed. Eighties music? That so-called golden era also gave us "Rock me Amadeus" by Falco and "Party All the Time" by Eddie Murphy. The halcyon days of high school? You were bullied mercilessly by the vapid "cool kids" and ate chicken burgers that were made of rat, the OTHER other white meat. The good old days your parents talked about? Those were hateful times for people of colour who were victims of unchecked and blatant racism, women had no autonomy over their reproductive choices, and anyone gay or transgender had zero legal right to express their love for their partner/s in public. Let's be clear. Things still have a way to go where we all enjoy equality and liberty but pining for a time that didn't exist is holding you back for appreciating what is now and taking action for what could be.

MY mother had her entire pubic area shaved before she had me via a vaginal cavity birth as it was "cleaner". Think about that for a second. I was born in 1971, and the medical system was feeding women shit about the "unclean nature" of their labia and Mons Venus. Do not let anyone feed you this line or similar malarkey. The Vagina is an incredible organ capable of self-cleaning, maintaining a delicate balance between acidic and alkaline. The Va-jay-jay takes action when recognising a foreign invader and making split section adjustments to accommodate size and girth including acting as a slippery dip for a baby to emerge through increasing to something like five times its average size. The Vagina can host the "G" spot and can produce lubrication that is almost unmatched by any synthetic equivalent. Basically, the Vagina and the surrounding labia is incredible and should be worshipped throughout all the lands. Knowing all this...act accordingly.

NEVER give more blow jobs than the oral sex you receive. In a non-academic study, I asked a bunch of lady friends, and the verdict was unanimous. Throughout our sex lives, we'd given more oral than we received. There are many reasons for this, but let's stop fucking about and start evening up the scorecard. And yes, Scorpio's keep a ledger. We notice shit like who goes down on who first. Who performs with enthusiasm versus under sufferance. And who's going through the motions rather than wanting their partner to enjoy themselves. Don't be a selfish lover or one who has resistance around dining out at the "Y". Ask your partner what they like and get down on it; just like Kool and the Gang implored you to do.

SOME fantasies are best left unfulfilled. Oh sure, the threesome you've fantasied about with your partner and the hot barista is steamy and all, but some fantasies are better in the head...and less so in the bed. For starters, the most sensual fantasies are centred on your pleasure: everyone present and accounted for is focused on your satisfaction and yours alone. Take that over to real, sweaty hot bodies, and you now have complex people in all their weirdness with competing needs, and yes, their desires that might not square with yours. In your fantasy, everyone is competing to give you the most incredible orgasm of your life. In real life, there's someone whose dick is refusing to be satiated, and you've been at this for 40 minutes and your neck's cramping. Look, I'm not saying to jettison the fantasy entirely—just be judicious in knowing what's best to remain as fantasy and what you can introduce into your "real life" sex life without your fantasy turning sour.

ANOTHER word about threesomes. Sure, they're the rage. But do pause to consider that by introducing another person into the dynamic might show you up to be the basic lover that you secretly suspect yourself to be. If you feel your skills and enthusiasm are on the wane, brush up on that shit before having a direct competitor wedged under your left buttock.

YOU must spend some part of your life as both single and living solo. This is not negotiable. It will be your secret weapon throughout your life knowing that as fucked up as shit gets in a cohabiting relationship or share house you can move all your items out using a horse float on a Tuesday afternoon without a word and live free and happy as a solo person. Needing no one, wanting for nothing.

EARN your own money. Marrying for money is a lazy and stupid financial plan. In every and all ways—back yourself.

NO. That's it. That's the perfect answer to the problem you were wrestling with.

DON'T be jaded or cyclical because it's fashionable. Employ critical thinking instead, and as the great philosopher of our time, Flavor Flav, reminded us, "Don't believe the hype."

YOU owe no one your time, your body, your attention, your money, your energy or your spirit. Any financial loans you have, pay down as rapidly as you can. Strive to live a debt-free life, and you will know true freedom.

DON'T talk AT people. You are nowhere near as fascinating as your parents led you to believe.

KINDNESS, always. Except if a motherfucker comes for you and then, by all means, cut them like a bitch.

BULLYING is different from critical analysis. Know the difference. It's popular to cry, "But I'm being bullied!!!" When you're rightly pulled up for hate speech, casual racism, white centring claptrap, and the like, hit pause baby doll and recognise there's a great chasm between people trolling you and people wanting you to grow through education, alternative views and FACTS. Be grateful that people want to see you grow into a better human by spending time correcting you and providing a path for growth. By all means block/delete/mute the trolls who want to grind on you and feed on their negativity. Stay open, however, for the good people who offer guidance, citations and way-finding through their own lived experience.

IF you're a white person living on indigenous lands, figure out the name of traditional land and research the traditional owners. It's not political correctness wankery, it's good fucking manners and is the very least you can do. Go an extra step and reference the name of the traditional lands you live on in address label. For example, in the "Address Field Line 2" I write "Cammeraygal, of the Eora Nation". Shit like that matters, be respectful and educate yourself.

ALSO, a white person, it's on you to learn more about white supremacy and how you've benefitted from the systemic discrimination of First Nations and people of colour. Consider it part of your energetic contract in being a good human in the world. Yeah, you're going to stuff shit up. I once gave a "Welcome to Country" rather than an "Acknowledgement of Country". (Sidebar: "Welcome to Country" is for indigenous people to welcome the non-indigenous people to gather on their land. I'm indeed the whitest person in Australia; my family of origin comes from an Anglo-Saxon background. So, it wasn't ok for me to give a welcome to country as I'm not indigenous). So be Ok with stuffing up, saying the wrong thing or mispronouncing words and phrases. It's good form to be open to outside criticism and commentary in order to learn, practise and grow. The only way to get better is to give it a red hot go. So, fire up that learning muscle and dive into examining your privilege.

JUST because they like you—doesn't mean you have to like them back. You are under zero obligation to reciprocate another's feelings. To thy own self be true and all that!

IF you go to an event and you're travelling in a pack, look out for the solo attendees and make a point of speaking with them. Turning up to an event by yourself is hugely confronting especially when it seems that everyone is arriving at the event like paired up animals marching two by two into Noah's Ark. Don't be a dick and go say hi. Compliment their shoes. Ask them what they're working on right now. Talk to them about a song or music they might be digging. It does not take much to be the kind and generous person that thinks of others. The costs are fuck-all, so be ridiculously loose in doling out kindness.

BE interested and interesting. Please resist the urge to talk about the weather or how someone got to the venue. Have some go-to questions at the ready to get to know someone. Have you ever tried yoga and if so, do you have a go-to pose? What have you read or seen recently that has interested you? What was the last thing that made you smile? Have you faced an existential crisis recently? Look, yes, the last one is my favourite as I'm a Scorpio and very shit at small talk. Let's just get to the marrow and kick on from there is my preferred mode of operation. But I get that not everyone wants to describe their inner-landscape within minutes of meeting. But just know if I meet you, I want to know what happened to you at eight years of age that had a transformative effect on your life.

IF you have the means, then it's your duty to share around the abundance—either financially or donating your time and skill to people that aren't doing so flash and causes that are close to your heart. And no, you don't have to post on the socials patting yourself on the back for donating time and resources—that shit is tedious and is part of the contract we enter as humans to take care of one another. No one wants to see your post about you fronting up to a charity ball in a new frock with a spray tan, coiffed hair up the wazoo, designer heels and stepping out of a Ferrari. ESPECIALLY when that charity ball would be lucky to pass on 5% of the taking once expenses and "appearance fees" are extracted from the pool of donated cash. Save yourself the dubious honour of being a social-climbing shitbird and donate the few thousand you would have blown on the clobber direct to the charity and stay at home to plot the demise of several of your secret enemies.

THERE'S a quote by Sun Tzu that you should abide by. "Wait long by the river for the body of your enemies to float by." I enjoy the generational aspect of revenge. Why deploy the full-blast of white-hot revenge when you can keep it on a low simmer for eons only to unleash in the most unexpected of ways in the most unexpected of times? There's your nemesis happily getting on with their life, and then fucking BANG! They awake to find the proverbial severed horse head is bleeding out on their velour bedspread. And don't let anyone tell you that revenge is wasted energy. That's usually said by some insipid piece who doesn't have the biscuits to follow through. Be the person who keeps their commitments and wait long by that river.

IT is not your job to make other people happy. Everyone is responsible for their happiness, and it is an incredibly shitty thing that some people do in outsourcing their joy to others. For example, you might feel pressured by a parent to keep stumping up year after year to attend family or religious events that have no meaning or value to you. Still, you begrudgingly attend, so you keep them happy. But at what cost to you? The entire world's population would be instantly more comfortable if we all learned that a. It's not our job to provide happiness for another, and b. Say a polite but firm no when people are trying to guilt you into something you'd instead not participate in. Oh, and if you're the person who guilts others into events and participation, knock that shit off. It's tiresome.

IN bad times, have a good time. It's no accident that the roaring 20's with the flapper dresses and the Charleston happened during the Great Depression of the 1920s. People need relief from the drudgery and the grind of everyday life. Now while donning a sequin dress and shimmying on top of the kitchen bench might not be your jam, seek out fun and joy in the everyday. Try absinthe. Go on a nighttime safari around your city with no destination in mind. Go and see some live gig of a musician you've never seen before. Wander in an art gallery, lingering over pieces you'd typically glide by. Invite a bunch of friends and almost-strangers around; ask them to bring a meal they love. Talk to strangers that catch your eye. Take up a hobby that's the opposite of your standard likes. Above all, enjoy yourself. None of us knows—well except for Scorpios, we tend to have a feeling for when we'll die—how long we have on this spiritual plane so stick your middle finger up at the bad news and marinate in all the lusciousness this world offers.

HE'S just not that into you. And that's ok. He's a sketchy dude—do you want that muppet to gird your loins?

BOOK the trip. Especially if it's to somewhere you've never been before. Travel opens up your eyes, world and your heart. Don't feel down if you can venture far. Some of my more memorable trips under Covid-19 restrictions of movement involved a nighttime urban safari around a nearby fancy suburb that I had explored as much as I desired to. The night involved an abundant haul at an independent book shop, Asian street food eaten on upturned milk crates and a nightcap at an ex-tittie bar. Pull-on your most fabulous strutting shoes and get amongst it.

IF you're not in therapy, we can't be friends. An unexamined life is just a waste of angst and exaltation.

TRENT Reznor and Patti Smith are the only deities you need worship. All others are false gods.

There are some people whose talent is otherworldly and for me—and you, if you're smart and know what's up—Trent and Patti are gods who mingle amongst us. I'm always interested to see what they're creating and over their long bodies of work, they have never fallen into ruts, into doing the safe thing and are using their art to challenge our thinking and societal structures.

SELF-DESTRUCTION is a waste of booze and drugs. And it's a boring cliche. Want to surprise yourself? Strive for growth and transcending your circumstances.

So much of what you beat yourself up for is the voice of a parent or a childhood bully. They are taking up real estate in your head. Turf 'em out with no notice of eviction. You are no longer a scared kid rendered mute. Reclaim your fabulousness and live a large, bold life.

BE grateful, be humble. This life could all vapourise in the time it took to read this sentence.

DON'T join a Multi-Level-Marketing (Relationship Marketing) scam. That shit is rank. And please spare me the nonsense about being great for women as it will allow them to grow a business authentically. Or to work from home so they can take care of their kids. Or give back to the third world communities that it strips resources from, pays pathetically and all this with the opportunity for uncapped earning potential. If the MLM product were that shockingly good, they would pay you a wage to sell it. MLM's pay zero entitlements. Unlike every other damn legit business worth its cojones, it doesn't offer sick pay or annual leave. It contributes zero to your superannuation, and in many cases, you have to buy the product as demonstrator kit before you can guilt a friend into listening to how AHMAZING the product is. You need to work all the hours God sends to be on the socials, sneakily contacting acquaintances from school days under the pretence of, "Hey, I was just thinking of you, and I wanted to give you this opportunity to try this product that has TOTALLY transformed my skin". If you're considering an MLM—please, for all things Shirley Manson, check out the financial disclosure document that shows the typical annual revenue for each level within the MLM—it's sobering reading. For example, for one MLM shilling essential oils, only 99% of the distributors earned more than $860 in their first year. "What's that?" I hear you ask, knowing that any business needs to get traction before being a raging success. Well, for other seasoned distributors, only the top 10% make more than $1,260. For the time you would spend on growing someone else's business via your "network," you could establish your own business and make bank. Or you could go to college and get additional skills that would mean a better paying job or a career you enjoyed rather than tolerated. Or you could even spend that time you would otherwise promoting that MLM shit by building your own Death Star on your dining room table. Because DEATH STAR over MLM any damn day.

DO not break stride. Keep marching towards that goal, a free-er life, your future self. Don't let any fucker create a detour by throwing down a speed bump or diversion in your path. Keep striding forward right over that barrier and diversionary person.

IN times of hardship, meditate on the only tarot card that matters: The Hermit. The card reminds you to be your own guru, to trust your intuition; that all you need is within you. And the only step you need to talk right now is the next one. Incidentally, the hermit would not be on social media so curb your time following "influencers" and messy bitches on those platforms in the hope they're providing the answers you're seeking.

I know the popular adage is to "follow the money" to unpick the threads of scandal, corruption and capitalism's worst ills. But I prefer to "follow the power". Power is more ancient, more enduring and more motivating than any amount of money. When you're trying to figure out what end game is any scenario—including the most benign office intrigue of "Why did Darryl eat the last Iced Vo-Vo when he's previously droned on about his celiac condition?" The answer is to follow the breadcrumbs and boulders left by those seeking power. It reveals everything.

STAY left. This advice applies to politics, roadways and footpaths in the Southern Hemisphere. The "stay left" advice is voided when creating art, delving into the esoteric and dressing to impress. Incidentally, if you're unsure of what to wear or the invite is a little vague on the dress code, I always find that the uniform of tight black T-shirt, black jeans and heels so high your nose bleeds has never done me wrong. Added bonus! It doesn't matter what gender you identify as, this advice is applicable.

YOU don't have to go. Even if you said, you would. Reserve the right to change your mind. Replace the Fear of Missing Out with, "Thank the gods I did not have to put up with Trevor's halitosis". Or Martin's savoury salad with marshmallows and Karen's incredulity that people might be finding Corona times, a little bit, you know, hard. She'll chirp happily at you that her life hasn't changed much significantly as she's closeted within the health service and spends most of her days avoiding work by skiving off to sell her homemade ceramic fairy figurines on Facebook Market Place. I put it to you; any night spent at home washing the cat and attempting a home tattoo of your own eyebrows will trump the night out with people you want to punch in the kidneys.

ALWAYS leave them wanting more. Be a charming guest, a scintillating presenter, an adoring Aunty, but for-the-love-of-all-things-cheesecakes, get the fuck out before everyone's attention span wanes, and your schtick gets older than dirt.

A little bit of mystery is a beautiful thing. Never has this been more applicable where it comes to the closed bathroom door when personal grooming, plucking, shaving and shitting is in play.

GO to events solo. You see, hear and absorb so much more if you don't have a companion as a crutch. You're free to make your mind up about a speaker or piece of art without parsing the views of someone else. Also, the chances of talking to an intriguing stranger are heightened, which will expand your mind or help you see things in a new light. If nothing else, say the event is a complete washout, you don't have to convince someone else to slink off to a nearby bar for a refreshing sherbet.

DRINK some water. Move your body. Smile at animals that you pass. Mentally bless the people you walk by on the street with all the abundance in life they are due. Smile when you make phone calls; people "hear" that smile through the line. Help someone or even yourself. Say thank you and mean it. That, right there, is a recipe for a good day.

KEEP the channel open. Twisting your poor brain to find a solution to a sticky problem? Go for a walk in nature, jump on public transport, flick on a radio station you'd rarely bother with or sit in a cafe and eavesdrop on nearby conversations. Without fail, I've used this trick and have found the solution to the issues I was wrestling with. Once, I was bereft of ideas for the design of a perfume bottle I was working. Nothing was landing, so I jumped on a Melbourne 6 tram and cruised the boulevard and fucking BOOM! Passing the forecourt of a commercial building was an impressive sculpture of granite, and from there, my brain slotted all the fragmented and frayed design pieces of my perfume bottle into a perfect whole.

YOU don't need to give up sugar. You need to give up your need to dampen your very valid feelings (Rage! Despair! Hopelessness! Envy!) with comfort eating of the sugary kind. Don't mistake me—sugary treats are a life force, but delve deeper into why you're reaching for a Cronut every time you hang up from your passive-aggressive father. That shit is telling.

NO one is coming. This is either the best or most devasting thing you've ever heard. By this I mean, you need to help yourself first before anyone else can assist. So many times, we give over our personal power to another loved one or stranger to "fix" us. And we're conditioned to do this! One day my prince will come, I'll get fitter when I meet someone, I'll look for a new job once my kids reach primary school...all the things we trade-off when we're hanging out for the first move to be made by another. What if we instead made the call to the rehab clinic? Or decided our physical health was a priority and sought out medical support to lose weight rather than wait for a friend to join us on a 28-day fitness challenge? Or that we booked the God damn solo trip to Guatemala rather than bribing our not-interested partner to tag along. Look, there's an avalanche of help and support for beautiful humans on the other side of whatever challenge your squaring off against, but it's on you to make your mark, take the first step or begin your Hero's journey.

DON'T let anyone tell you there's no such thing as failure. There most certainly is. It's common within the entrepreneurial space to produce inspirational posters set against the backdrop of a breaching whale proclaiming, "Fail fast and forward". How quaint. What these self-appointed business gurus fail to tell you – apart from the only business experience they've had was taking a commerce elective in high school – is that failure has very real and devastating consequences. In business, failure can mean loss of jobs, injury or even death to workmates or bankruptcy. In business, you MUST do all you can to avoid these failures. If you want to define failure in the business space as "I tried this idea and it didn't work out" or "Yeah, this prototype is a bit of a hot mess," then have at it. But be clear: leaving a decimated workforce through constant "restructuring," owing trusting investors shedloads of cash or having a workplace marked with death and injuries to your workers is nothing to champion. And it's certainly not something to offer as a reputation-builder keynote.

RINGFENCE your values. If you're a trusting type, then don't hang with the grifters who are on the take. Value freedom above all else? Then don't settle for a life with a clingy partner that wants you to "settle down". If you want a life of breathless adventure, why did you just sign up to an eye-watering mortgage because you're under pressure to accumulate assets by your family? You say you want a partner that will treasure and care for you, so why is that you're marrying that douche you know has been stepping out on you? Compromise on colour choice for the bathroom, on what you'll order for dinner and what you'll call your kid. But never compromise your values, you'll live a half-life and be an utterly miserable twit.

You're not done yet.

You're not broken, you're beautifully human.

I believe in you.

The last thing you need is to take the advice you never asked for, but I hope you have found something of value in here to remind you of yourself and how powerful you are.

Even for a non-Scorpio.

Songs that Scorpios groove to.

Except we don't groove – we simmer.

Please enjoy these tunes that also beautifully complement the life advice previously given.

Because I know you'll be tempted to listen to some auto tune crap masquerading as credible music, here's the link for the accompanying soundtrack to living your best life, despite not being a Scorpio

https://tinyurl.com/y5ok3mwq or on Spotify look for "Life Advice from a Snarky Scorpio

"Trust is Rust" Adalita

"No Excuses" Alice in Chains

"Don't Waste My Time" The Angels

"Fashion Bleeds" Archers of Loaf

"Rock Steady" Aretha Franklin

"Pattern Against User" At The Drive In

"Fight Outta You" Ben Harper

"Hound Dog" Big Mama Thornton

"Army of Me" Bjork

"Heart of Glass" Blondie

"He War" Cat Power

"Yellow Bird" Clairey Browne & The Bangin' Rackettes

"Up for it" Henry Rollins

"Doll Parts" Hole

"Old Fitzroy" Dan Sultan

"Policy of Truth" Depeche Mode

"Sixty Minute Man" The Dominoes

"Last Cup of Sorrow" Faith No More

"The Bad in Each Other" Fiest

"Let Me Down Easy" Gang of Youths

"Push it" Garbage

"You Played Yourself" Ice-T

"Humble" Kendrick Lamar

"Hooch" Kelis

"Wheelhouse" Kurt Vile

"Norman Fucking Rockwell" Lana Del Ray

"Phenomenal Woman" Laura Mvula

"River" Leon Bridges

"Darkness" Leonard Cohen

"Juice" Lizzo

"Bound for the Floor" Local H

"Dreamin" Lou Reed

"Naked Eye" Luscious Jackson

"Sabotage" Beastie Boys

"I'll Be Ready" Mama Kin

"Ode to Sad Disco" Mark Lanegan Band

"Move With Me" Neneh Cherry

"Chaos" New Yong Pony Club

"The Mercy Seat" Nick Cave & Bad Seeds

"The Line Begins to Blur" Nine Inch Nails

"Dancing Barefoot" Patti Smith

"Dance of the Clairvoyants" Pearl Jam

"Good Fortune" PJ Harvey

"Like Clockwork" Queens of the Stone Age

"Portion for Foxes" Rilo Kiley

"Final Form" Sampa the Great

"L.E.S. Artistes" Santogold

"S.U.C.C.E.S.S" by Tim Rogers and the Bamboos

"Parabola" Tool

Love You's and Fuck You's

Big love to Lindsey and Alex and the entire Tiny Book Course team for being so awesome and running a course where you actually produce something rather than gather digital dust. If you feel you have a book busting to get out, start with a Tiny Book and register for upcoming courses here: www.tinybookcourse.com

Much respect and heart-shaped Memojis to the songwriters, artists and bands who provided the soundtrack to the writing of this Tiny Book.

I would have never written this book without the accompaniment of Red Rock's Lime and Black Pepper Chips and Smith And Shaw's Sav Blanc. And unless you've knocked out a book—don't judge the menu choices.

Fuck you to Donald Trump and his band of shifty grifters. This seems as good as any forum to say that.

Fuck you also to the peeps posting and promoting conspiracy theories that link the Coronavirus with Bill Gates, The Pope, some child pornography ring run out of a Washington Pizza Bar, Microchipping humanity, 5G, The Illuminati, the music of Nickleback (I might have thrown this one in here for kicks), the Clintons and Tamagotchis. I mean...come the fuck on. Why spend your time tieing your brain in knots weaving together a baseless set of circumstances together when there are ample causes like the gross inactivity on Climate Change and the continuous wilful disregard of indigenous rights and calls for justice. I mean, why tackle those real and urgent problems when you can yell all day on the socials about "SHEEPLE" and "BUT HER EMAILS" and "DO YOUR RESEARCH". Honestly, this level of ignorance and lack of critical thinking is criminal.

And a final fuck you to the International Astronomical Union that reclassified Pluto as a dwarf planet. Dwarf, my arse.

About the Author

Fiona Jefferies is a 12th House Scorpio Sun with a kicky Scorpio Ascendent. She lives in Sydney, Australia, and spends her nights doing urban safaris, arguing with herself about the best Nine Inch Nails tune and making the most wicked, slutty brownies.

Her first book was "A Small Book About Suicide" and the last concert she saw was Tool's Fear Inoculum which was strangely predictive of the pandemic times we're currently living in.

Fiona like grainy toast with lashings of vegemite, striking the triangle (Trikonasana) pose when under duress and a tall redwood named G.

www.ingramcontent.com/pod-product-compliance
Lightning Source LLC
Chambersburg PA
CBHW020331010526
44107CB00054B/2071